Social Skills Printables Workbook:
For Students with Autism & Similar Special Needs

By: S. B. Linton
AutismClassroom.com

© 2019 by S. B. Linton.
www.autismclassroom.com

All rights reserved.

This book may not be reproduced, stored in a retrieval system, or transmitted by any means electronic, mechanical, photocopying, recording, or otherwise, without written permission from the author.

Table of Contents	Page
Self Management	4
Self Management	5
Self Management Checklist	6
My Own Self-Monitoring Checklist	7
Reinforcement Assessment 1	8
Reinforcement Assessment 2	9
Reinforcement Assessment 3	10
Information is "POWER" Cards	11
It's OK to Make a Mistake	12
Social Skills	13
Emotions	14
Match to Same - Emotions	15
Sad	16
Happy	17
Scared	18
Angry	19
Point to the Emotion Cards	20
Identify Emotions	21
Emotional States	22
Emotions – Match to the Same	23
Tell this Story	24
What Are They Feeling?	25
I Need a Break Lesson	26
Working Around Others	27
Taking Turns	28
My Turn Your Turn	29
Waiting	30
Sharing Space-Color by Code	31
Share	32
Sharing Vocabulary	33
Volume Control 1	34
Volume Control 2	35
Trace Words	36
Working With Others Word FIND	37
Self-Awareness	38
About Me…These Things Hurt My Ears	39
About ME…These Things Hurt My Eyes	40
About ME…These Things Hurt My Skin	41
About ME…These Smells Hurt My Nose	42
About ME…These Things Hurt My Feelings	43
Making a Mistake	44
Not Getting What You Want	45
Stress	46

Social Skills Printables
By: Autism Classroom

autismCLASSROOM.com

Table of Contents (cont.)…	Page
Calming Down	47
Coping with Challenges	48
Self-Awareness Words	49
Describe a Feeling	50
What Is He Saying?	51
Emotion APPs	52
Friends Graphic Organizer	53
What is a Friend?	54
Communicating with Others	55
Thank You	56
What do I like the best?	57
Social Skills Vocabulary	58
Saying Thank You	59
When to Say Thank You	60
Class Rules Narratives	61
Imitate Others	62
I Want This, What Do I Do?	63
I Don't Want This, What Do I Do?	64
Repeat, More & Again	65
Game Rules	66

Social Skills Printables By: Autism Classroom

A Little About the Social Skills Printables Workbook…

The Social Skills Printables Workbook: For Students with Autism & Similar Special Needs will work well for any students whose special needs include developmental delays or they may work for younger students in primary grades learning to develop social skills. The worksheets can supplement a social skills curriculum or they can be used daily as a discussion starter for reviewing social skills. This workbook includes social skills related worksheets that require variations in response styles for many answers. (Ex. matching, cutting, circling, and pasting.) The skills are broken up in to 4 sections: Self-Management, Emotions, Communicating with Others and Self-Awareness.

Self-Management

Self Management

It is important to pay attention to your own actions.

What is Self-Management?

Taking responsibility for my own behavior.

Thinking about what other people do.

Self Management Checklist

Practice tracing the checkmarks.

Write a checkmark in each box.

☐ Do my work.
☐ Follow directions.
☐ Stay seated.
☐ Use an inside voice.

Social Skills Printables

7

Name_____

My Own Self-Monitoring Checklist

Create your own self-management checklist. Cut and paste 4 skills you want to monitor.

☐	
☐	
☐	
☐	

Hands to self.	Look forward.
Follow directions.	Work quietly.
Quiet voice.	Keep my pencil still.
Inside voice.	Keep my hands in my work station.
Stay in my seat.	Focus on my work.
Keep my feet on the ground.	Answer questions.
Do my work.	Participate in class.
Use my words.	Slow down and complete my work.

Social Skills Printables   Name_____

Reinforcement Assessment 1

Color or mark the things you like to do.

Social Skills Printables 9 Name_____

Reinforcement Assessment 2

Color or mark the things you like to use.

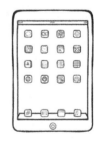

Social Skills Printables

Reinforcement Assessment 3

Color or mark the things you like to eat.

Social Skills Printables

Name_____

Information is "POWER" Cards

Draw a line to match the picture to the card.

Following Directions

Super Hero Man likes moving fast. He thinks you should move fast too. Especially after your teacher asks you to do your work. He loves to complete a work task when he is asked.

Lining Up

Do you know who likes to line up? Dewy the Dino does! He thinks that kids that line up without touching others in line are awesome. When Dewey the Dino lines up he never touches the other dinosaurs. He knows that he has to keep his dino hands to himself.

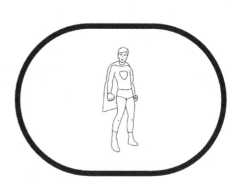

Sharing

Princess Polly wants me to remember these things when playing.

1. Share my toys.
2. Say please.
3. Keep my hands safe.

Social Skills Printables 12 Name_____

It's OK to Make a Mistake

Julie made a mistake. Help her correct her mistake. What are some good options for her if she makes a mistake?

| Cry and yell. | Raise her hand to ask for help. | Use her eraser. | Say it's ok. Then, keep trying. |

| Throw the paper away. | Play with her toy instead. | Figure out a different way to solve it. | Blame others. |

Social Skills Printables   Name_____

Social Skills

Directions: Color in the social skills words with rainbow colors.

take turns

share

smile

hello

please

Emotions

Social Skills Printables

15

Name_____

Match to Same - Emotions

Directions: Cut on the dashed line. Match the pictures that are the same.

Cut.

Social Skills Printables | 16 | Name_____

Sad

Directions:
Find the words below in the word search.

f	f	s	c	r	y
e	s	a	w	f	f
m	a	d	b	p	r
r	d	n	b	g	o
u	s	e	c	w	w
u	p	s	e	t	n
r	i	s	h	t	s

cry   sadness   mad
frown   upset   sad

Social Skills Printables

Happy

Directions: Circle the pictures that show a happy face.

Mark the word happy.

happy   sad   goat   happy
book   happy   pencil   happy

Social Skills Printables

Scared

Name_____

Directions: Draw a line to match the letters in the word scared.

s	e
c	d
a	r
r	a
e	s
d	c

Mark the word **scared**.

orange   scared   light   scared   beacon   scared   other   top

Social Skills Printables   19   Name_____

Angry

angry

Definition:

Hostility or displeasure.

Directions: Circle the correct word that matches the definition.

| danger | calm | angry |

WRITE IT !!!

angry

Mark the word angry.

other   angry   blink   angry
angry   red   angry   book

Point to the Emotion Cards

Point each emotion card. Match the word with the picture.

scared

shy

angry

excited

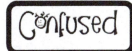
confused

sad

happy

worried

Social Skills Printables

Identify Emotions

Name_____

Today at school I feel...

fearful

silly

sad

happy

angry

nervous

tired

confused

My emotion is

_____

Emotional States

Directions: Cut on the dashed line. Match the words to the pictures.

Cut.

happiness

sadness

anger

fear

Social Skills Printables

23

Name_____

Emotions – Match to the Same

 fear

 anger

 sadness

 joy

Social Skills Printables 24 Name_____

Tell this Story

Directions: Which sentence tells about this picture the best.

| A | The students are happy. |
| B | The students are worried. |

What Are They Feeling?

Directions: Which sentence tells about this picture the best.

A	The kids like playing in the slide.
B	The kids seem to be worried.

A	The boy is feeling sad.
B	The girls are running to the store.

A	The students are playing baseball.
B	Something scary is behind the door.

A	Something has made him feel angry.
B	The boy is feeling joyful.

Social Skills Printables

Social Skills Printables

Name_____

I Need a Break Lesson

Directions: Cut out the pictures below. Glue them into the appropriate box to tell how to ask for a break.

Yes

Correct Way

No

Incorrect

 run away

 cry

 raise my hand

 fall on the floor

 earn tokens

 use a break card

 do my work

 push someone

Working Around Others

Taking Turns

Directions:
Dot a circle with another person. Take turns after each dot.

Social Skills Printables

My Turn Your Turn

<u>Directions:</u> Dot a circle with another person. Take turns after each dot. Use the pictures at the bottom to show "my turn" and "your turn."

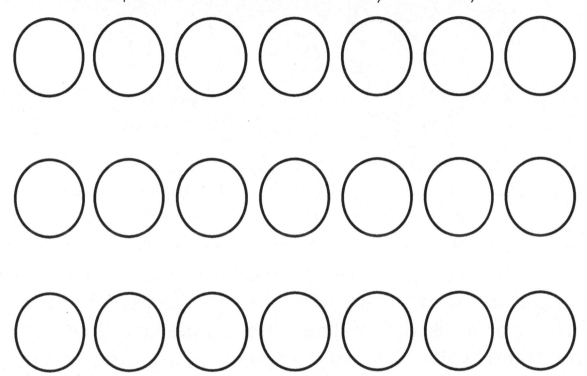

Social Skills Printables

Name_____

Waiting

Teachers: Read this passage to the students.

These kids are waiting in line. Waiting is remaining still and non-active in expectation of something. Waiting is hard because sometimes there is nothing to do while you wait. Sometimes people choose the wrong thing to do like bump into the person in front of them or walk out of line. These kids are doing the right thing while waiting. They are standing in line. They are keeping their hands to themselves. They are quietly waiting for instructions from the teacher.

What are some things you can do when you wait?

Listen for instructions

stand in line

sit quietly

KEEP MY HANDS AND FEET STILL

Think of something fun

Look for a toy

CRY AND GET UPSET

Sharing Space
Color by Code
Directions: Color by the code.

LOOK FOR	DO
2 girls sitting next to each other.	Color their hair brown.
2 boys sitting next to each other.	Color their hair black.
A girl with a ponytail sitting next to a boy.	Color her hair yellow.
The girls sitting nearest to the teacher.	Color their chairs green.
The boy sitting in the middle.	Color his chair blue.

This page is intentionally blank due to an activity on the next page.

Share

Mark the word.

give	share	share	ear
share	share	stack	share

Paste the word.

share

Cut and paste in the right column.

share share

share share

Social Skills Printables

Sharing Vocabulary

Name_____

Directions:
Match the definition to the words.

share	
friend	
please	
thank you	

- To let another person take part in what you have or what you are doing.
- A phrase to show your appreciation.
- A nice way to ask for something.
- Someone you like to be around.

Social Skills Printables 34
Name_____

Volume Control

Directions: Give a number to each volume level.

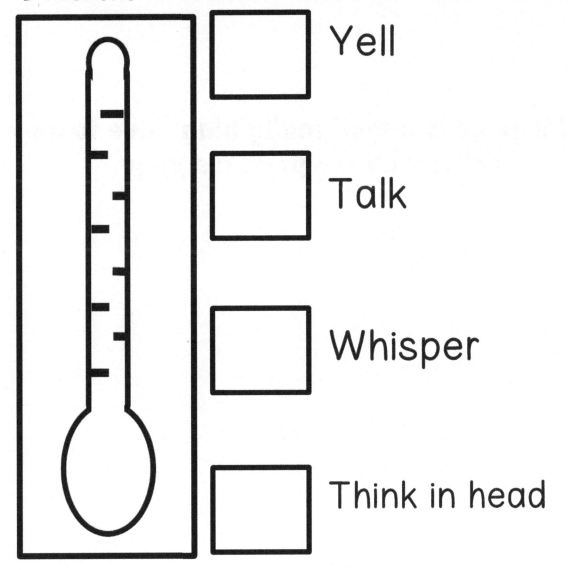

☐ Yell

☐ Talk

☐ Whisper

☐ Think in head

[3] [2] [4] [1]

Social Skills Printables

Volume Control 2
Places to Use Volume Levels

Yell	Talk

Whisper	Think in your head

Social Skills Printables

Name_____

Trace Words
Directions: Trace over these words.

take turns

share

volume

listen

wait

Working With Others
Word FIND
Directions: Circle the words.

share
- share
- leaf
- care
- shoe

listen
- sand
- listen
- make
- bell

take
- green
- look
- deep
- take

wait
- bait
- meet
- wait
- hair

turns
- turns
- shirt
- hat
- dot

volume
- pen
- mat
- volume
- van

Self-Awareness

About Me... These Things Hurt My Ears

Directions: Mark the items that hurt your ears.

Pictures shown: crying-phone-thunderstorm-yelling-computer-insects-fireworks-headphones-earbuds

Social Skills Printables

Name_____

About ME...These Things Hurt My Eyes

Directions: Mark the items that hurt your eyes.

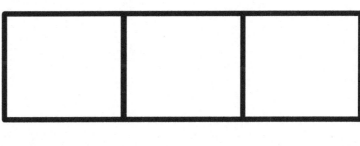

bright Light

bright colors

flash light

fireworks

laptop

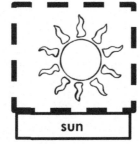
sun

screens

nothing

About ME...These Things Hurt My Skin

Directions: Mark the items that hurt your skin.

Pictures shown: pencil-shoe-fork-someone touching me-washing hands-sock-wind-shirt/sweater-hugging-no picture here

Social Skills Printables   Name_____

About ME...These Things Hurt My Feelings

Directions: Mark the items that hurt your feelings.

- ☐ People leaving me out.
- ☐ Someone grabbing me.
- ☐ Friends working with me.
- ☐ Mean words.
- ☐ Seeing that other students are worried.
- ☐ When students are happy.
- ☐ Not getting a turn.
- ☐ It is not on the list.

Social Skills Printables Name_____

Making a Mistake

Directions: Circle what you can do if you make a mistake.

Social Skills Printables

Not Getting What You Want

Trace the word.

Patient

Draw a line to the same letter in the word patient.

| p | a | t | i | e | n | t |

| t | n | e | a | p | t | i |

When you do not get what you want, what should you do?

| be patient | cry |
| fight | make cookies |

Which student is being patient?

Stress

Draw a line to match the letter on the top to the letter on the bottom.

Circle the picture of what can you do when you feel stress?

Social Skills Printables   Name_____

Calming Down

Circle the words that say "calm" in this picture.

Discuss some ways to calm down when you are upset. Draw a picture of a way that you can calm down.

Mark the picture that shows someone being calm.

Point to each number to practice a clam down strategy:

1
2
3
4
5
6
7
8
9
10

Social Skills Printables

Name_____

Coping with Challenges

What does it mean to cope?

☐ To see something in a different way.

☐ Handling problems or responsibilities in a calm or appropriate manner.

☐ To tantrum, scream and cry when dealing with difficult activities.

☐ Breaking down and giving up.

Directions: Tell which boy is coping well with the change in his schedule?

Self-Awareness Words

Trace the words. Color the pictures.

hurt

stop

too loud

break time

Describe a Feeling

Directions: Cut and paste 2 sentences that describe each feeling.

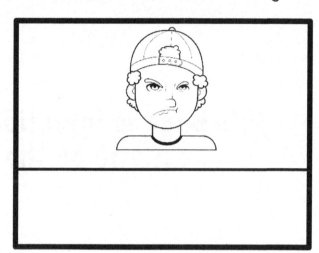

I feel sad.	Wow, I'm shocked!
I am angry.	Yes. I love this.
Today is a great day.	This is frustrating.
I am surprised.	Why can't I have one?

What Is He Saying?

Directions: Trace over these words then color the picture.

Emotion Apps

Directions: Point to the letters on the keyboard to spell the words.

- ANGER
- CALM
- TIRED
- JOY
- SADNESS
- FEAR

Friends Graphic Organizer
What do friends do?

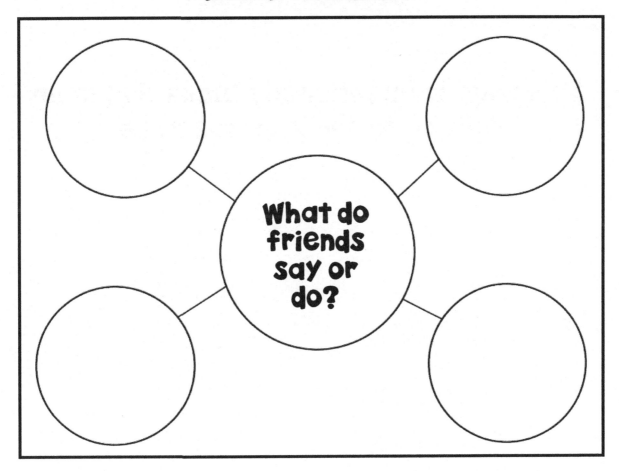

Social Skills Printables

What is a Friend?

friend

Definition: A person you like talking to, like playing games with or like being around.

DIRECTIONS: Color in the word that that means that you are acting like a friend.

friendly   scared

SPELL IT:
friendly

| l | d | n | f | e | r | i | y |

Communicating with Others

Color in the word.

thank you

Is this a good way to say thank you?

○ Yes
○ No

○ Yes
○ No

○ Yes
○ No

How would you use communication to say that you liked something?

○ Say thank you.

○ Say I want more.

○ Look the other way.

WRITE IT !!!
thank you

Fill in the circle for the words "thank you."

○ talk

○ thought

○ thank you

Social Skills Printables

What do I like the best?

I like _____

because _____.

I don't like _____

because _____.

Choose three pictures. Cut and paste them in the sentences above.

puzzles | drawing | playing with a friend | the playground | working at a desk

music | it's loud | it makes me dizzy | being in a crowd | I'm shy | it makes me happy | I get messy | it's fun

Social Skills Printables   Name_____

Social Skills Vocabulary

Directions: Cut out the definitions and glue them into the correct box.

play	
friend	
buddy	
lunch bunch	
greeting	

- A group of people who eat lunch together.
- Another word for a friend.
- To do an activity for enjoyment.
- A person who you enjoy being around.
- Saying hello when you see someone.

Saying Thank you

Thanking other people is a kind gesture. It shows that you appreciate what the person has done for you. When you are happy at what someone did you can use sign language, pictures or words to say "Thank you."

Directions: Color in the 3 pictures that show times when you should say thank you.

You get a present from a friend.

Someone tells you an easier way.

Someone helps you.

Someone is mean to you.

Color in the words "thank you."

I can say, sign or show thank you.

Social Skills Printables

60

Name_____

When to Say Thank You

Directions: Cut and paste the pictures in the correct box.

Say thank you	Do not Say thank you

help   a gift   a fight   teasing   reading to you   computer time

Social Skills Printables

Class Rules Narratives

Directions: Cut on the dashed lines. Match the picture to the correct rule.

I will try to keep my hands and feet safe.

I will try to do my work.

I will try to listen to what my teacher says and do what my teacher says.

I will try to use an indoor voice when I am inside.

Imitate Others

Imitate Motor Movements
jog

Directions: Ask the student to "Do this" while jogging in place.

Imitate Motor Movements
arms up

Directions: Ask the student to "Do this" while putting your arms up.

Directions: Circle the words that mean imitate.

play   copy   say
pencil   do this book

Directions: Draw a line to show the steps to imitating others.

 Think about what they are doing.

 Look at the person.

 Do the same thing.

I Want This, What Do I Do?

Directions: Cut on the dashed lines. Match the yes and no to the correct way to show that you want something.

| ASK FOR THE BALL USING WORDS, PICTURES OR SIGN LANGUAGE. | CRY AND FALL TO THE FLOOR BECAUSE YOU COULD NOT GET THE BALL. |

Yes   No

I Don't Want This, What Do I Do?

What are 2 ways you can respond if you do not want to do something?

I can say no thank you.

I can say maybe later.

I can yell and scream.

l	a	t	e	r	m
e	s	h	w	f	a
m	m	a	y	b	e
r	d	n	o	g	b
u	s	k	u	w	e

Find the words in the word search.

thank you   maybe later

Repeat, More & Again

Trace the words.

| repeat | more | again |

Mark the words **repeat, more & again**.

seat	play	run	repeat
play	more	game	door
fun	stop	again	less

Sue had fun and she wants the activity to continue, what 3 things can she say?

- More
- Repeat
- Stop
- Again

Game Rules

Directions: Draw a line from the rule to the picture.

| Share. | Wait for your turn. | Be a good sport when you win. |

Directions: Check the 2 boxes that the boy should say if he loses the game.

☐ Good game.

☐ Maybe next time.

☐ I don't like this game.

THANK YOU FOR YOUR PURCHASE.

AutismClassroom.com offers books and resources for Special Education and General Education. We make materials to bring out the best in your students with autism and similar special needs.

Website - www.autismclassroom.com
Teachers Pay Teachers Store - www.teacherspayteachers.com/Store/Autism-Classroom
Pinterest - http://www.pinterest.com/autismclassroom
Instagram - http://instagram.com/autismclassroom
Facebook - https://www.facebook.com/pages/Autism-Classroom/30958373294?ref=hl

SPECIAL THANKS.

Thanks to the following artists for their wonderful clip art and fonts.

Educlips
Rossey's Jungle
Jessica Stanford Fonts
KB3 Teach
Dancing Crayons

CHECK ONLINE FOR MORE PRINTABLES FROM AUTISM CLASSROOM.COM

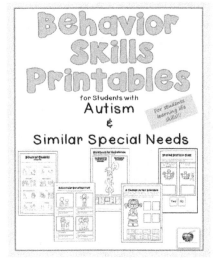  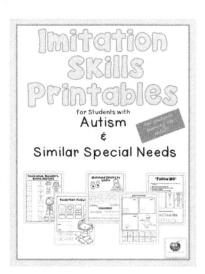

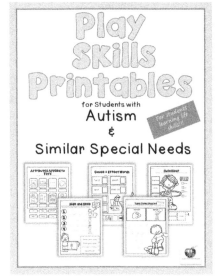 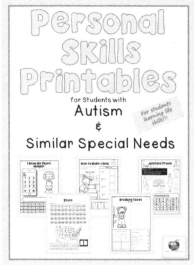 

CHECK ONLINE FOR THE SOCIAL SKILLS INTERACTIVE BINDER FROM AUTISM CLASSROOM.COM

NOTES:

Made in the USA
Coppell, TX
26 February 2023

13444323R10057